May God richly bless you
this coming year. Remember
to depend on Him as your
Strength and Guiding Light.
For He has promised to care
more for you even than He
does for the birds.

~ Do not worry.... He is
your Provider

♡ Chelsea Webb
'05

DEDICATION

To the Rev. and Mrs. S. F. Collier
Because I want to say "God bless you" for your splendid
work amongst the destitute of Manchester. —MGP

GOD'S CURE *fo*

BY

MARK GUY PE

━━ ≡◆≡ ━━

"Consider the lilies of the
How they grow;
They toil not, neither do the
And yet I say unto you
That even Solomon in all his
Was not arrayed like one of
Take therefore no thought for the
— from Matthew 6

REPRINTED BY

DAVID WILKERSON PUBL

PREFACE

A book on worry must needs be written with care. Thank God, there is a blessed Gospel for busy men and burdened women, but it must be a Gospel that is fitted for their moments of leisure. Whatever it may lack at the hands of him who brings it, there must not be wanting sympathy, interest, homeliness. This has been my thought, my aim, my prayer in writing this book.

The homeliest of ills, I have sought to deal with it in homeliest fashion. To make it the more complete I have added such hymns as seemed likely to set forth its teaching more fully; for there is a soothing in the lilt and rhythm of words as well as in their sentiment, for which a jaded soul is often grateful.

For the use of Miss Rossetti's poem, I have to acknowledge my indebtedness to Messrs. Macmillan. Of the hymns, I cannot find that any permission is required for their use. If I am mistaken I must ask forgiveness and will hasten to correct the error. The chapter headed "Consider the Lilies" was for the most part published some time ago in another form.

— MARK GUY PEARSE

FOREWORD

I am a lover of old classic books written by our spiritual fathers. My daughters often help me find these rare gems—browsing old bookstores and Internet book auctions. When my daughter, Bonnie, laid a copy of "CHRIST'S CURE FOR CARE" on my desk I picked it up, thinking I would skim through it and return to it again later for a comprehensive reading.

I could not put the book down. It was so compelling and healing. It was dedicated to a Rev. and Mrs Collier, who ministered to the destitute on the streets of Manchester, England, at the turn of the 20th century. I found the book to be so inspired I passed it on to a few trusted friends who were also deeply moved by its message. They confirmed what was already impressed on my heart by the Holy Spirit: This book must be reprinted.

It is with pure delight that we bring back this treasure to be shared with the body of Christ. Though written nearly 100 years ago, it is even now more relevant than when first published. Here you will find deeply spiritual truths that will be eagerly devoured by those who battle fear, worry, distress and anxiousness.

The prophet Jeremiah admonished God's people to seek out "the old paths" to find rest for their souls. You will find rest for your soul, mind and body within these pages. This rare classic is a gem, a pearl, a heavenly medicine for the worried mind.

— DAVID WILKERSON

GOD'S CURE FOR WORRY

The text of this book, originally published
under the title *Christ's Cure for Care*,
has been determined to be in the public domain.
It has been reprinted in its original form,
retaining the British grammar and style.

Unless otherwise noted, all Scripture
quotations are from the Authorized
King James Version of the Holy Bible

ISBN 0-9709326-3-4

CONTENTS

24 No man can serve two masters: for either he will hate the one, and love the other; or else he will hold to the one, and despise the other. Ye cannot serve God and mammon.

25 Therefore I say unto you, Take no thought for your life, what ye shall eat, or what ye shall drink; nor yet for your body, what ye shall put on. Is not the life more than meat, and the body than raiment?

26 Behold the fowls of the air: for they sow not, neither do they reap, nor gather into barns; yet your heavenly Father feedeth them. Are ye not much better than they?

27 Which of you by taking thought can add one cubit unto his stature?

28 And why take ye thought for raiment? Consider the lilies of the field, how they grow; they toil not, neither do they spin:

29 And yet I say unto you, That even Solomon in all his glory was not arrayed like one of these.

30 Wherefore, if God so clothe the grass of the field, which to day is, and tomorrow is cast into the oven, [shall he] not much more [clothe] you, O ye of little faith?

31 Therefore take no thought, saying, What shall we eat? or, What shall we drink? or, Wherewithal shall we be clothed?

32 (For after all these things do the Gentiles seek:) for your heavenly Father knoweth that ye have need of all these things.

33 But seek ye first the kingdom of God, and his righteousness; and all these things shall be added unto you.

34 Take therefore no thought for the morrow: for the morrow shall take thought for the things of itself. Sufficient unto the day [is] the evil thereof.

CHAPTER I

The
TEACHER
and HIS
TEXT

*And He opened His
mouth, and taught them.*

ST. MATTHEW 5:2

✥ *The* TEACHER *and* HIS TEXT ✥

S THE LORD JESUS CHRIST WENT FORTH UPON HIS ministry how great a contrast He must have felt between Himself and everyone about Him. Think of one man in the world, and that a poor man, with many sorrows, who never knew what worry meant—one man who walked this earth ever with an utter freedom from anxiety, who lived a life of perfect and absolute trust in God.

All around Him there was fretting, overeagerness, worry, fear. The lives of men were dwarfed by anxiety about the commonest matters. He moved amidst crowds of people who were worrying themselves to death as to how they should live, unfitting themselves to enjoy anything by their anxiety lest they should have nothing to enjoy. And out of that overeagerness came selfishness that grew by all it gained, and covetousness that ate like a canker into the soul. And His own life was all calm and sunshine. These bitter ills of anxiety and covetousness never touched Him.

This ignorance of worry on His part might seem to unfit Him to speak of worry to others. It is, therefore, the more needful for us to see clearly how perfectly qualified is the Good Physician to deal with this curse of worry. There are men and women, gifted, wise, benevolent, who yet are not always wise enough to know that they are unfitted to talk to other people about resignation. I can think of nothing more irritating than for the minister, rotund and ruddy, with the ring of robustness in his voice, and everything about him proclaiming how well to do he is, preaching to some burdened woman or hungry man the duty of contentment. Let my Lady Bountiful, brilliant with jewels and rustling in her silks, bring her beef-tea and jelly by all means to the sick, and send her hot-house grapes to the fevered sufferer. In so doing she shall do well. But let her breathe no word about the blessedness of a contented spirit.

He who speaks with authority here must have gone along the desert way. He must have learned in poverty the art of pity. He must have found in loneliness and want the sacred sympathy which soothes and strengthens the soul beset with worry.

This is Christ's fitness to talk to us of worry, that He Himself met in every condition the worries of our humanity and conquered them by trust in God.

He was ahungered. And to Him hunger meant all that it ever meant to any—a gnawing pain, the craving of every vital power for its sustenance, the trembling weakness, the dizziness of brain, the utter exhaustion of every faculty of body and mind and heart. Then to Him came the tempter—*"If Thou be the Son of God command that these stones be made bread."* There stood the Christ, white-faced and worn, and calmly spake His unfaltering trust in the Heavenly Father. That was His stay, His strength, His triumph.

Think of Him going on His way alone, past the home where the wearied labourer sat amidst the happy family and blessed God for the simple evening repast. Think of Him as the sun sank behind the western hills, and the bird flew to its shelter within the nest, and the fox crept to its home beneath the rocks. Stillness lay on the villages where the households slept in happy safety. But He went through the night weary, homeless, hungry, cold. (The Son of Man had not where to lay His head.)

Again, think of Him asleep in that wild night at sea, the darkness of the night adding to the peril and fear of the fishermen. There is the wild howling of the winds, while the waves leap like living things impatient for their prey, hissing, raging, foaming in their madness, and He amidst it all asleep. And when they wake Him He rises, and beneath His outstretched hands the waves sink, hushed, and winds are silenced instantly, as if abashed that they had dealt so roughly with their Lord. The disciples, we read, were astonished at His power. But He was astonished at their fear. *"Why are ye so fearful? How is it that ye have no faith?"*

Filled with all this holy calm, with heaven in His soul, the Lord Jesus looked forth upon men dragged down and cursed by worry. And all within Him longed to bring them into a true relationship to God. Wrong with God, the man was wrong with everything, with himself and with all the common things of daily life. How shall the world be brought into its true position, and how shall men and women come to share this supreme blessedness of the Saviour? Here, and here only, is the answer: By the revelation of the Father.

Turn for a moment from the Lord Jesus to another teacher, the Apostle Paul. He comes up from all the bondage of the law and the pride of the Pharisee, up as Jesus Christ came down from the clear light of His Father's presence. In all its setting and method, its shape and colour, how different is the Sermon on the Mount from the Epistle to the Romans. The seventh chapter of that epistle is the cry of a great soul struggling to be perfect, to fulfil its own ideal. He writhes as in the folds of some serpent, its venom in his veins—*"Oh wretched man that I am!"* Then in the eighth chapter comes the burst of his deliverance. The tyranny is broken and the soul is free, and the Apostle coming upward from the tyranny of the law, finds his escape in the truth which Jesus Christ sets forth in the Sermon on the Mount—*"We have received the spirit of adoption whereby we cry Abba, Father."*

There are many ways in which we may think of God. He is the Creator; the Almighty power which sustains the universe; the All-wise directing it; the Most High demanding the obedience and service of His creatures. He is the Judge before whom we must appear. But none of these can ever satisfy us. If I am to love God, if I am to trust Him I must know Him in some other way. He must come to me by myself; He must meet me in the separateness of my own soul and enter into its secret chambers. To commune with me He must know me, not as the All-knowing, but as one gracious and pitiful, able to understand my wants, to help my weakness and to forgive my sins. And more than that—knowing me through and through, all that is false and selfish and mean, yet must He love me, love me with a simple kindliness and patient love that shall embolden me to open all my heart to Him. There is but one aspect, one knowledge, one relationship of God which can satisfy us. It is that which the Lord Jesus Christ sets before us in these words: *"Your Heavenly Father."*

In the religious life it is not too much to say that everything depends upon our thought of God. It is everything for us to find out how the Saviour would have us know God.

Some men think it is necessary for us to have grim and terrible thoughts of God. They say it makes strong Christians. Perhaps it does, in the same way that the Indians make strong children by killing all the weak ones. Twenty must die that one may live. Oh, blessed is it to turn and listen to the gracious words which proceed out of the Saviour's mouth. He who knows my needs as no other does, He who knows my sins as no other does, He who knows God as no other does, comes to tell us of the Almighty. Come and let us learn how Jesus Christ would teach us of Him. The Saviour leads His disciples to the mountain top. Seated here, what shall be His chosen emblems of the Most High? Of old the Psalmist had sung—*"The Lord God is a Sun."* Surely of all created things this was the fittest image of the Almighty, the light and life of worlds, glorious in itself, measureless in its might, boundless in its beneficence, inexhaustible in its supply, pouring out incessantly its generous fullness.

Then again, about them rose the hills, the chosen emblems of the Everlasting. But the Lord Jesus stooped and picked a flower—a flower of the field. *"Here learn of God,"* said He, *"Its maker is your Father. If He so clothe the grass of the field, shall He not much more clothe you, oh, ye of little faith?"*

Then Jesus stayed a moment as if listening. There rose the lark with rapturous song, soaring toward the sun, and from the rocky heights came the croaking of the raven.

"Behold the birds," said He. *"Your Heavenly Father feedeth them. Are ye not much better than they?"*

Yet remains one further emblem that brings God nearer still. We can think that in the crowd were many children, and some little one, gazing into that face and listening to that voice, with child-like simplicity comes to His side. The hand is tenderly laid upon the child, the arm is set about him, while, turning to the crowd, Jesus said: *"What man of you if his son ask bread will he give him a stone? Or if he ask a fish, will he give him a serpent? If ye then, being evil, know how to give good gifts unto your children, how much more shall your Father which is in Heaven give good things to them that ask Him?"*

A bird, a flower, a little child—these are the voices that are to speak to men of God; all that is glad, all that is beautiful, all that is trustful and loving, all that tells of tenderness and constant mercy—these are Christ's chosen emblems of the Most High.

Your Heavenly Father. Here are four great and blessed truths that we may take to the innermost heart.

1. I have not to understand great mysteries. How easy it is to be overwhelmed by the thought of God. To some, indeed, it may seem impossible not to be overwhelmed by it. How we may perplex our brains and vex our souls with theories and theologies, and creeds and definitions, until God is lost to us in a maze and mist of words. Your Heavenly Father—that I can accept, and there I can rest. The little

child lies in the mother's arms, ignorant indeed—all that it can do is to delight in that ministry of love. It unlocks chambers of the heart and claims them for its own, which the wise and prudent never knew. By the infinite gentleness and patient help of the mother to the child, God would make Himself known to us. Stretch forth to Him the helpless hands, lift up to Him the longing eyes. About us, nearer and more constant than anything else, sure as the round world beneath our feet, vast and glorious as the great Heaven above us, is the love of the Heavenly Father. That first—if God is my Father, I have not to perplex my soul with awful mysteries.

2. The next blessed truth is this—If God is my Father, I have not to make Him love me. His love is mine for ever and ever, fixed and unalterable in the very nature of God. Think of the little child that has to try and make the mother love it. Poor little thing! It must not tell when it is hungry, or cry when it is sad, or shriek when it is frightened. It must be always trying to be bright and beautiful to win the mother's love! No, that love must go before everything, it must underlie everything, it must watch for the commonest wants, anticipate them, and find its joy in ministering to them. Even our sins cannot undo the love of the Father; can, indeed, only reveal the height and depth and the strength of that infinite love that is ours for ever and ever.

"When he came to himself he said: How many hired servants of my father's have bread enough and to spare, and I perish with hunger? I will arise and go to my father: And when he was yet a great way off his father saw him, and ran and fell on his neck and kissed him." Linger over the vision until the heart glows with the wonder of it all—the love that longed unwearied, that waited, that watched, that ran in its eagerness of welcome, that could not do enough to show itself. All this is ours, yours and mine, for ever and ever in Him who is our Heavenly Father.

3. Your Heavenly Father. Then all that He is He is for me, and all that He has He has for me. How wonderful is this relationship. Here is a man waited on by his servants, his want and pleasure met by skillful hands, artists that paint for him, authors that write for him, a host that add to his safety; those who bring him fruit and food and flowers. And here amid them all is the little child, without any sense, without any skill, who brings no gain, who adds nothing to the master's greatness or wealth, and yet this little one is more to the father than anyone else. Others touch the master at this point or that, but all that he is belongs to the child, and all that he can be. Others bring their work or wares, and get their wages. But this little one brings nothing, yet possesses all. *"All that I have is thine,"* says the father, glad for the child's sake.

Your Heavenly Father. Think of it, dwell upon it, until the gladness of it fills and thrills the soul.

4. Your Father which is in Heaven—Then He understands and knows how best to train me for the highest life and to turn me to the best account, for within us is another nature with wants to be supplied and capacities to be developed, which only God Himself doth understand.

Every day bring His love afresh into the life. Open the shutters and draw up the blinds and let this love stream in upon the soul like the light of the morning. Every day surrender yourself afresh to His gracious helpfulness and gentle guidance. It is along this way we must go to learn the lesson that the Lord would teach as He seeks to cure our worry.

OH LORD, I WOULD DELIGHT IN THEE
St. Leonard

O Lord, I would delight in Thee,
And on Thy care depend;
To Thee in every trouble flee,
My best, my only Friend.

When all created streams are dried,
Thy fulness is the same:
May I with this be satisfied,
And glory in Thy name.

Why should the soul a drop bemoan,
Who has the Fountain near—
A Fountain which will ever run
With waters sweet and clear?

No good in creatures can be found,
But may be found in Thee:
I must have all things and abound
While God is God to me.

O that I had a stronger faith
To look within the veil;
To rest on what my Saviour saith,
Whose word can never fail!

He that hath made my heaven secure,
Will here all good provide;
While Christ is rich, can I be poor?
What can I want beside?

O Lord! I cast my worry on Thee!
I triumph and adore;
Henceforth my great concern shall be
To love and please Thee more.

CHAPTER II

The MASTER'S
COMMAND

Therefore I say unto you,
Take no thought for your life.

ST. MATTHEW 6:25

ᚔ *The* MASTER'S COMMAND ᚔ

HIS IS THE COMMANDMENT OF THE LORD JESUS Christ to those who count themselves His disciples. Be not anxious. In the old version it reads *"Take no thought,"* but the word *thought* has changed its meaning and we must change the word.

It was said of Queen Mary that she died of thought about Calais. People do not die of thought today, although they sometimes die for want of it. The word meant that Queen Mary died of fretting, worry. Even the words *"Be not anxious"* are scarcely enough to express it fully. It means that sulphuric acid which eats into the vitals of a man. So we may take it. Therefore I say unto you, Do not worry, Do not fret, Do not be distracted.

Now at the outset let us think of this as the Gospel of Jesus Christ. We are apt to make the Gospel very often a little shallow thing compared with that which is set forth by the Lord Himself. With very many the whole of the orthodox Gospel is a matter of having their sins forgiven and then going to Heaven when they die. There are hosts of good people who have nothing whatever to do with God except in the confession and forgiveness of sin. I have known people who could not ask a blessing at dinner without the mention of their sins. The Lord Jesus said very little about having our sins forgiven and still less about going to Heaven when we die. This certainly is a part of the blessed Gospel, a great part, but it is only a part.

The Lord Jesus Christ would have us think of His salvation as a force within us that makes the man master of things, the master of circumstances. Listen to the exultant boast of St. Paul: *"In all these things I am more than conqueror in Him that loved me."* That is the Gospel of Jesus Christ. The finding of an authority that sets the man in his right position towards everything with which he has to do.

Because this is forgotten we have no conscience on the matter of worry; we do not think of it as wrong; we never confess it even as a failing, much less ask forgiveness of it as a sin. If the preacher were to say Do not steal, or Do not kill, we accept the word at once as of divine authority. But if the preacher should say Do not worry, there springs up instantly a sense of resentment. Everybody knows the kind of feeling that meets such a counsel. "Ah! It is all very well for you to talk," as if the authority were that of the preacher only, and not of the Master Himself. Who is not familiar with the angry mutter: "Let anybody live where I live, and put up with the things that I have got to endure!" That settles the matter in the opinion of a great many. But mark from whom this word comes: *"I say unto you"*—with Him this matter must be settled, the Lord and Judge of all men.

How familiar we are with another plea: "Well, but you see, I am naturally of a very worrying disposition."

What of that? What is the meaning of the Gospel if it does not turn a man's disposition from what it is to be? Think of a prisoner brought before a judge for stealing. The judge turns to him sternly: "You have stolen these things. What have you to say for yourself why judgment should not be pronounced upon you?" "Well, my lord," replies the prisoner, "you see, I am naturally of a very acquiring disposition."

Then says the judge: "You and your disposition must go to prison." My disposition is no excuse for my offence. My disposition will not save me from condemnation for my sins.

Now shall we free ourselves from all reserve, and let this word come to us with the force of the Lord's own authority. Knowing us as we are, knowing us as we should be, knowing all the circumstances of our daily life, all the patience and faith that we may require, He saith: *"Be not anxious."* Let us earnestly and prayerfully surrender ourselves to this command.

The first Counsel is this:

DO NOT WORRY BECAUSE YOU DO WORRY.

Whilst we are ready enough to excuse ourselves, we are also apt sometimes to be content with crying out against ourselves: "Well, yes, I know—this is my failing, I am so anxious, I do so fret and worry. I wish it were not so." And thus we spend our energy in fretting because we fret and worrying because we worry.

All this shall avail us nothing. Homeopathy may have its place, but it will not cure worry. You cannot cure worry by worrying about it. It is well for us carefully to consider with what exquisite graciousness the Lord Jesus deals with this evil. In all His character there is nothing more beautiful than to see Him as Master of the art of reproof. The hardest thing in the world is to reprove wisely. In nothing need we take more care when dealing with others than in the matter of reproof. We may scold people into hell, but we can never scold anybody into Heaven. We may scold people from delusion into despair, but we can never scold them from failure into hope.

Linger for a moment on this aspect of the Saviour's character. On one occasion there was a great quarrel amongst the disciples; so fierce was it that even as they came along the road the noise of their wrangling was borne upon the breeze to the ears of the Lord Jesus. *"What was it,"* He asked afterwards, *"that ye disputed amongst yourselves as ye came along the way?"*

They had disputed which of them should be the greatest. How it must have hurt the heart of the meek and lowly Saviour to find this spirit springing up amongst these fishermen, this lust of superiority. Think what it must have meant to Him who made Himself of no reputation, and took upon Him the form of a servant, and became obedient unto death, even the death of the Cross. We well might expect to see all the indignation of the Lord Jesus Christ stirred to its utmost depths.

But what does He do? He sits down. There is a great deal in that. You cannot be very fierce or demonstrative when you sit down. Silently Jesus beckons a little lad to come and stand at His side. The presence of that little one took away all harshness. Everything was filled with a beautiful tenderness as, with His arm about the lad, Jesus said: *"Except ye become as a little child ye shall in no wise enter into the Kingdom of Heaven."*

So is it when the Lord Jesus comes to deal with our worry. He who Himself marvelled that the disciples should be frightened or anxious even amidst the fierceness of the stormy sea, fetches in the birds and bids them sing to us and charm away our worry, even as the musician of old drove forth the evil spirit by the sweet strains of his harp. He brings in the flowers and by their beauty and their fragrance He heals this sickness of the soul, as the physician finds in the plant the healing balm.

We must be careful to hear throughout all these words this undertone of tenderness. I sat one day by the bedside of a sufferer who was about to undergo an operation. Her face lit up as she said: "I never knew before the meaning of that word—is there no physician there? He is the good physician, not the surgeon." How blessedly true it is. He brings only the balm. It is bad enough when any seek to cure their own worry by worrying about it, but it is a great deal worse when we try to cure the worry of others by worrying them. Here the hand that binds must be careful not to bruise. Here that which is meant to heal may so easily inflame. So is it needful to be rid of any tone and touch that can irritate. They who dress this wound must be careful to disinfect themselves of poisoned germs.

COMMIT THOU ALL THY GRIEFS

Paul Gerhardt, 1656
Translated from German by John Wesley, 1739

Commit thou all thy griefs
And ways into His hands,
To His sure truth and tender care,
Who heaven and earth commands.

Who points the clouds their course,
Whom winds and seas obey,
He shall direct thy wandering feet,
He shall prepare thy way.

Thou on the Lord rely,
So safe shalt thou go on;
Fix on His work thy steadfast eye,
So shall thy work be done.

No profit canst thou gain
By self-consuming care;
To Him commend thy cause, His ear
Attends the softest prayer.

Thy everlasting truth,
Father, Thy ceaseless love,
Sees all Thy children's wants, and knows
What best for each will prove.

Give to the winds thy fears;
Hope, and be undismayed:
God hears thy sighs, and counts thy tears,
God shall lift up thy head.

Through waves, and clouds, and storms,
He gently clears thy way:
Wait thou His time, so shall this night
Soon end in joyous day.

━━◆━━

CHAPTER **III**

The TWO
MASTERS

No man can serve,
two masters...Ye
cannot serve both
God and mammon.

ST. MATTHEW 6:24

⟿ *The* TWO MASTERS ⟿

CHAPTER III

LET US TAKE ONE BY ONE THE REASONS BY WHICH THE Lord seeks to cure this ill of worry. He might be content to command us only, but He seems to say with infinite graciousness: *"Come, let us reason together."*

It will be well for us to recall the scene—how they sat of old with the Master on the mountain top, underneath the open heavens, the beauty of the flowers on every side, and the singing of the birds about them. Far below was the blue sea of Galilee, nestling between the hills, the groups of villages clustering along its shores. The whole scene was one of beauty. Let us seek to enter into such an atmosphere, so charmed.

And still more, let us seek the attitude of the disciple sitting at His feet and listening to the gracious words which proceed out of His mouth. The natives of South Africa take their wounded up the mountain height and lay them there, finding that the purer air holds some healing power that is lacking in the lower lands. On the mountain where the Master sits and talks we may find a cure for all our ills.

No man can serve two masters. The word "serve" is a sterner word than we know how to render today. There is but one word in the Bible for service, and that is slavery. The servant is always the slave. Work was a degradation of old, and is yet wherever the name of Jesus Christ is not known. It is told of some Oriental sovereign who was watching a game of cricket that when he heard many of the players were rich men, he was amazed and turned to ask of those about him, "Why don't they pay some poor people to do it for them?" Almost every working man in the world was a slave until Jesus Christ came into it. He by His own toil has uplifted and transformed service from a degradation into a nobility. Now, the shame is not in work, but in the neglect of it. There are but two classes today, working-classes and paupers.

So we must read it. *"No man can be the slave of two masters, for either he will hate the one and love the other, or else he will hold to the one and despise the other. Ye cannot be the slave of God and mammon."*

━━ ━✦☰ ━━

What then is mammon? Money? No indeed. Oftener it is the want of it. Most of us fret a great deal more from the want of money than from having it. Mammon is whatever a man frets about.

The moment I fret about a thing I am its slave, instead of its master. And there is no slave-master in the world like worry. Another master may work you fourteen hours a day, but he must give you time for sleep. Another master may grudge the dinner hour, but sometime you must eat. But worry will work you twenty-four hours a day and spoil your appetite in the bargain. And if you sleep, what a burdened, broken sleep it is—as Hood puts it with his grim humour:

> *"Fretful by day,*
> *At night to his own sharp fancies a prey,*
> *He lay like a hedgehog rolled up the wrong way,*
> *Tormenting himself with his prickles."*

This is the first great curse of worry. When we fret we put the good thing in the wrong place. It is our master instead of our slave. And this is the only sin there is, putting the good thing in the wrong place. There is no bad thing in the world. God made everything that is, and said of all: "Behold, it is very good." The apple in paradise was a good apple on the tree; a horrible apple in the hand ; and a cursed apple in the mouth. It is ever so. The devil cannot make things, he is not wise enough. He can only unmake. He is

Apollyon, the Destroyer; all he can do is to put the good thing in the wrong place. Lord Palmerston said of dirt: "It is good matter in the wrong place." That is a capital definition of dirt. Thank God for dirt—in the right place. If there were no dirt there would be no potatoes. But in the wrong place it is a plague, a mischief, a source of a thousand ills.

Nothing can put the world in its right place but for us to be in our right place, and this in the meaning of Christ's Gospel. He my Lord, and I the lord of all things because He is mine. He my Master and all things my servants for His sake.

It is well to set beside this aspect of worry the words of the Saviour in the parable of the Sower. The history of a seed lies in three little words—in, down, up. It must get in or it cannot get down. It must get down or it cannot get up. It must get up or it cannot get ripe.

The first failed to get in—that was a waste of good seed, so far as it was trodden under foot, yet that which the fowls of the air devoured was better than wasted. But in any case there was no waste of soil. We have no right to expect corn to grow on the highway; it is not meant for it. We do not look for corn even on Cornhill or bread in Bread Street.

The next got in, but it did not get down, and it withered away. Again the loss of good seed, but not the loss of good ground.

Where nothing else will grow, we cannot expect to grow corn.

But then comes the sadness of the story, where the seed got in and got down, but it never got up. There was the waste of good seed and of good ground. The waste of man's toil and honest effort, and of God's earth and God's sunshine and God's shower. Where thorns grow there corn should grow, for there is depth of earth.

How well we know these people. They come to church; they listen with intelligence, interest, sometimes with eagerness, and delight. They are quick to see a point, and to seize it, and respond in glad agreement. They have plenty of brains, plenty of earnestness, plenty of response, but there is no fruit. The thorns spring up and choke it.

What are thorns? They are mammon—the things men worry about and fret about. Thorns are capital things in the right place. A farmer would as soon have a fence of thorns as of anything—it keeps the cattle in and it keeps the cattle out. But thorns in the wrong place are a torment indeed. The bramble king is of all kings the greatest plague and the least profit. My boy said to me a good thing one day, when we were in the country. He had a prickle in his finger: "Father," said he, "a thorn in the hand is not worth two in the bush, is it?"

Note well how the Lord Jesus Christ describes these thorns. Not the world. It is God's world and not the devil's, and is a grand world in the right place. God made the man at the first with the world under his feet, but sin turns things upside down, and the man has got the world on top of his back. That is why most of us stoop so. We stagger like Atlas, without his strength indeed, but beneath his burden. God gave the man dominion over the world, but sin gives the world dominion over the man. It is the worries of this world of which the Master speaks—they are the thorns, not riches. Do not let us abuse in words that which all of us would like to have if we could.

"Ah, my dear madam," said a minister one day to a friend of mine, "it is a dreadful thing to have one's heart set upon money."

"Yes," said she, "but it is a capital thing to have your hand on some."

That is precisely the difference. A good thing in the hand, it is a horrible thing in the heart. Not riches is it that are condemned, but the deceitfulness of riches. How stern and startling is the picture which the Apostle sets before us of riches beckoning the man further and further into the bog, sinking deeper at every step until the cold, foul waters close over his head. *"Having food and raiment, let us be therewith content. They that will be rich fall into temptation and a snare, and into many foolish and hurtful lusts which drown men in destruction and perdition. For the love of money is the root of all evil."*

Not other things is it, but the lusts of other things of which the Master speaks—it is the strength of the soul, the energy of the heart, the thought of the life being absorbed in these things. Then do the thorns strike their roots deep in the soil, and they rise up with fierce strength and flourish, and underneath them the good seed is choked and becometh unfruitful. So nothing comes of the better thoughts; the Sunday purposes are slain by the Monday's worries— *"The thorns grew up and choked it."* Thorns—it is the same word that is used when the soldiers plaited a crown of thorns, which they thrust upon the Saviour's head. But they who are the slaves of worry wear the thorns in the heart.

I heard a simple Cornish miner once utter a prayer that it were well for us to offer every day: "Lord, save us from overeagerness about the things of this life." That is the truth that underlies the whole discourse. Be not overeager. So might it be rendered perhaps as best interpreting the phrase—"Taking thought." Or we may render it as being distracted, the attempt to serve two masters whose wills and commands are utterly antagonistic. We read of the archangel Michael and the devil contending for the body of Moses, but in a sorer plight is he who seeks at once to be the servant of God and mammon. Therefore I say unto you, Be not overeager.

There are creatures that take the colour of that on which they feed. The character of the man is made by that on which the heart is set. Therefore saith the Saviour: *"Where your treasure is, there will your heart be also."* Wisely has some German written, "The heart which is created only for God is dishonoured and degraded if set on things which perish. We turn the heart into a moth."

We are to find in the Lord Jesus Christ a power that makes us master of things. And yet more, much more than that. We are to find in Him the true purpose and service of things. Upon him who is right with God all things do wait, and minister with splendid service, enriching him with the finest gold. *"All things work together"*—a great unity knits all things, one great purpose lives and throbs in all—*"All things work together for good to them that love God...that we be conformed to the image of His Son."* As in the story of the Babe of Bethlehem, the wise men led on by the star in the Heaven come with laden camels and troops of attendants to lay before the Holy Child their gold and myrrh and frankincense. Where Christ dwells there all things in Heaven and earth do bring their fullest, richest, best. Every loss is made a greater gain in likeness to our Lord; every gain becomes yet more than gain in gratitude and fuller service; every sorrow working out a deeper sympathy, the graciousness of a readier pity, a wiser helpfulness; every joy bringing a fuller music of praise, the life made richer in thanksgiving.

This is the divine philosophy. The man who was the servant of things, their slave, becomes their lord and master, and they wait on him and bring their golden gifts and loftiest service.

Therefore I say unto you, Be not anxious.

MY SPIRIT ON THY CARE
Henry F. Lyte, 1834

❦

My spirit on Thy care,
Blest Saviour, I recline;
Thou wilt not leave me in despair,
For Thou art Love Divine.

In Thee I place my trust,
On Thee I calmly rest;
I know Thee good, I know Thee just,
And count Thy choice the best.

Whate'er events betide,
Thy will they all perform;
Safe in Thy breast my head I hide,
Nor fear the coming storm.

Let good or ill befall,
It must be good for me;
Secure of having Thee in all,
Of having all in Thee.

━━✦━━

CHAPTER IV

L~IFE~ *and*
I~TS~ W~ANTS~

Therefore take no thought
saying, What shall we eat?
or, What shall we drink?

ST. MATTHEW 6:31

⇥ LIFE *and* ITS WANTS ⇤

HEREFORE I SAY UNTO YOU, BE NOT ANXIOUS ABOUT YOUR
life, what ye shall eat or what ye shall drink; nor yet for your
body, what ye shall put on. Is not the life more than meat, and the body
thán raiment?"

Let us notice carefully what this does not mean. It is a
source of constant mischief that we talk about the world as if it
were the devil's and not the Lord's: a world in which
everything that belongs to it is an ill and a peril. Some have
interpreted these words "Be not anxious" as if they mean that
we are to have our minds so set on things above that all things
of the earth are nothing to us. We are to drift along our way
accepting what comes in this world and putting forth all our
energies to grasp at the other world. This is to lose the whole
meaning of the message. As long as we are in this world we
shall have a life and shall need the meat to sustain it; we shall

have a body and shall need clothes to wear. As long as we are in this world there is a mouth to be fed; and we must find a bed to lie on and a roof to cover us. There is something mean in canting about the world as if it were a plague or a peril, and then we cheerfully go home and get our dinner off it!

He who does not do his duty in this world will never do his duty in any world. He who does not do his duty to his brother will never do his duty to his God. I am bound to put my whole strength and energy and wisdom into my business. To be lackadaisical, half-hearted, so taken up with things above as to be slipshod in my dealings with things below, is neither to serve God nor man; neither to serve this world nor the next. Because I am a Christian I am bound to be earnest and indeed enthusiastic in all that makes for the welfare of the place in which I live, and of the people about me, and of the nation to which I belong. He will never do his duty as a Christian who does not do his duty as a citizen. I am unworthy of my liberties unless I seek to extend to others the good that has been conferred upon me. Surely there is nothing more cowardly than that which seems to say—"This is the victory that overcometh the world, to run away from it!"

Let us see then what the words do mean. It is as if the good Lord reasoned with us.

"My child," He seems to say, "hast thou a life?"

"Yea, my Lord."

"And whence didst thou get that life?"

"It is indeed Thy gift."

"Then if I have given thee thy life, do not I pledge Myself therewith to give thee that on which thy life depends? *Is not the life more than meat?*"

Let the argument sink down into the depths of us. If God Almighty has taken upon Himself the responsibility of bringing us into the world, He has accepted the responsibility of sustaining us as long as we are in it. He is a faithful Creator, complete in all His works and perfect in all His ways. What should we think of a mother who said to her baby, "There, I have given you your life, now you must take care of yourself." A mother! No, a murderess! The faithfulness of our God is the very foundation on which the round world is builded, the force that holds it together. Mark this faithfulness providing for the creatures at the beginning in the very order of creation—first the light and then the home; first the supply and then the creature that finds all waiting for it; first the sea and then the fish; first the grass and then the cattle; first the Paradise and then the man.

"Is not the life more than meat?"

Think of the mystery of life.

It is God's own secret. The life is the breath of God. We hear the sound of it, and see the signs of it, but we know not whence it cometh or whither it goeth. Our life binds us to the Author and Giver of life in a relationship more close and more

51

wonderful than any relationship on earth can set forth. The father accepts and meets the claim of his child. The mother finds in the care of her little one a joy that the angels might almost envy, a solace for every suffering, a recompense for all weariness and watching; her service repaid a thousandfold in such fine gold as no other hand can bring, the mystery of motherhood made complete by that supply of sustenance in which from her own bosom she gives her life for the life of the child. The God that made a mother is the great Father whose highest and fullest joy is to minister to the life that He has given. Yet with us the father and mother do but transmit the life. God is the great source and origin of it all. What height and depth of mystery, what a world of claim and what a pledge of supply lie in those words, "The Author and Giver of life."

Wholly dependent as we are on God for the beginning of life, let us remember that we are no whit the less dependent on Him for the sustaining of that life. It has been pointed out with great force that if the vital actions of a man's frame were directed by his will, they are so minute and complicated that they would immediately fall into confusion. The action of the heart, the circulation of the blood and the course of the vital functions are caused through means and by laws which are not dependent on our will and to which the powers of our mind are altogether inadequate. Had our life been in our keeping, a doubt, a moment's pause of irresolution, the forgetfulness of a single action at its appointed time would have terminated our existence. Every heartbeat is the mysterious bidding of our God, a thing apart from our will and our control. The life which He has made so dependent upon Himself, carries in itself the pledge of sustenance.

"Is not the body more than raiment?"

Here again the Master seems to appeal to us.

"Hast thou a body, My child?"

"Yea, verily, my Lord."

"Didst thou come by it by any thought of thine?"

"Nay indeed, my Lord. Thou hast fashioned it with all the mystery of brain and heart, of nerve and strength. These subtle energies are Thine."

"Then, My child," saith He, "if I have given thee a body, have I not thereby pledged Myself to give thee raiment wherewith to cover the body? Do I send forth the birds without feathers, or the beasts without fur? Do I not wrap the very buds in their brown overcoats until they are ready to open in the full sunshine? Therefore I say unto you, Be not anxious."

How much we lose for ourselves and for others by always talking about our souls and forgetting our bodies. As Professor Drummond has reminded us, in reality Christ never said "Save your soul." It is a mistranslation which says that. What He said was "Save your life." God is the Maker of the man, body and soul, and He cares for us not in bits and patches, but in all and in everything. The body that He has made so wonderfully is redeemed from destruction as much as the soul and is cared for as much as the soul. It is as men and women that He knows us, not as souls, and it is in the whole round of life that He holds us dear to Himself, not in solemn moments now and then. God cares as much for us in the world as in the Church; as much for a man in a workshop as for a man in worship. As much for a woman in a pantry as in a prayer-meeting; as much for us in our business and pleasure as in our devotions.

"Is not the body more than raiment?" Think of its mystery. Stretch forth your hand and move the supple wrist. Think of the score of hinges on which its movements turn. Ask the cleverest mechanic you know to make a hinge that can turn a dozen ways at once. Ask him to work it by some noiseless energy unfailing, stored up and waiting for use almost without effort, often without consciousness.

"The human hand," says Sir Charles Bell, "is so beautifully formed, it has so fine a sensibility, that sensibility governs its motions so correctly, every effort of the will is answered so instantly, as if the hand itself were the seat of that will; its actions are so powerful, so free, and yet so delicate, that it seems to possess a quality instinct in itself; and there is no thought of its complexity as an instrument, or of the relations which make it subservient to the mind; we use it as we draw our breath, unconsciously, and have lost all recollection of the feeble and ill-directed efforts of its first exercise. Is it not the very perfection of the instrument which makes us insensible of its use?"

And this is no less true of every part of the human frame. Everywhere there is the same infinite skill, the same perfect adaptation, the same noiseless energy. That which God hath fashioned so perfectly, shall He not graciously cover and protect? *Is not the life more than meat, and the body than raiment? Therefore I say unto you, Be not anxious.*

THROUGH ALL THE CHANGING SCENES OF LIFE
Nahum Tate and Nicholas Brady, 1689

Through all the changing scenes of life,
In trouble and in joy,
The praises of my God shall still
My heart and tongue employ.

Of His deliverance I will boast,
Till all that are distressed
From my example comfort take,
And charm their griefs to rest.

O magnify the Lord with me,
With me exalt His name!
When in distress to Him I called,
He to my rescue came.

The hosts of God encamp around;
The dwellings of the just:
Deliverance He affords to all
Who on His succour trust.

O make but trial of His love;
Experience will decide
How blessed they are, and only they
Who in His truth confide.

Fear Him, ye saints, and you will then
Have nothing else to fear;
Make you His service your delight,
He'll make your wants His care.

WHAT *the*
BIRDS SING
to US

*Behold the fowls of
the air: for they sow not,
neither do they reap,
yet your heavenly
Father feedeth them.*

ST. MATTHEW 6:26

✦ WHAT *the* BIRDS SING *to* US ✦

I T IS A PLEASANT THING TO KNOW THAT THE LORD JESUS heard the birds that we count to be our English birds. We think of Him standing and listening to the rapturous music of the lark, listening as it soars into the sunlight until hidden in the height, listening till the very song dies in the distance. We are glad He heard the cuckoo, the herald of our summer; that He heard the piping of the thrush and the rich notes of the nightingale. Pleasant is it to think that He knew the sparrow that comes to see us even in our great cities. *"Behold, behold,"* saith He, *"the birds of the heaven, that they sow not, neither do they reap, nor gather into barns."*

St. Luke places these counsels upon worry as immediately connected with the stern parable of the Lord in which He condemns the curse of covetousness. This gives altogether a new impressiveness and force to the words. Godet points out that all the figures from nature employed in reference to the fowls of the air seem to be connected with the foolish rich man—Sowing, reaping, storehouse, barns. *"The ground of a certain rich man brought forth plentifully. And he reasoned within himself, saying, What shall I do because I have not where to bestow my goods? This will I do: I will pull down my barns and build greater, and there will I bestow all my corn and my goods. And I will say to my soul, Soul, thou hast much goods laid up for many years; take thine ease, eat, drink, and be merry."*

This takes us back to the incident out of which this parable grows, where one comes to the Lord Jesus, asking Him to bid his brother divide the inheritance. *"And Jesus said: Take heed and beware of covetousness, for a man's life consisteth not in the abundance of the things which he possesseth."*

Covetousness is the sin of which Jesus Christ spoke more earnestly, more solemnly, and more constantly than of any other. *"Take heed and beware of covetousness."*

Here is its terrible illustration—it is independence of God. *"Thou sayest, I am rich and increased in goods, and have need of nothing."* Then comes the terrible and tragic ending of it all. *"God said unto him, Thou fool, this night thy soul shall be required of thee; then whose shall those things be that thou hast provided?"* It is in utter contrast with the rich fool that the Lord Jesus sets the birds. They neither sow nor reap, they have neither storehouse nor barn. Therefore are they more dependent upon the Heavenly

Father's bounty and afford the greater opportunity for the Heavenly Father's care.

"Your Heavenly Father feedeth them." Underline the word in your Bibles and underscore it in your hearts— *"Your Heavenly Father feedeth them."* Not their Heavenly Father. Their Maker, but your Father; their Master, but your Father.

The picture that rises before me as I think of these words is of a farmhouse where the mother comes with the basin in her hand, while at her side there stands the little maiden watching the fowls that gather and scramble for the scraps that are thrown to them. Do you think the little one ever looked up and said, "Mother, you have fed the chickens but you have forgotten to feed me"? Never. The little one had her breakfast first, and then the chickens had what was left. *"Your Heavenly Father feedeth them."*

This is the next argument. Think how many creatures there are in the world that have all the things we fret about without any fretting at all. It is sometimes hard indeed to be otherwise than anxious about the daily bread, but that is all the more reason that we seek the cure for worry which is ours in Jesus Christ. Dependent for our life on the daily bread, unable to control the future, with many possibilities of ill that threaten us, with lives about us dearer than our own, it is natural, very natural, that we think anxiously about the daily bread. And more than natural, it is a duty to think of it. There is a word strong and stern spoken by St. Paul, that he who doth not provide for his own house is worse than an infidel. To the man who eats his last crust, to the woman who grudges the slice as she cuts it. God knows how tenderly this word must be spoken. For such here is a sweet message—*Your Heavenly Father careth for you.*

The Master bids us when we pray say, *"Our Father, give us this day our daily bread."*

OUR FATHER—is it not in itself a cure for worry? Speak it over softly and lovingly in the heart. Whence think you comes our pity for the children and our worry for them but from the great heart of Our Father in Heaven? And He teaches us to pray *"Give us this day our daily bread."* He is not so all taken up in the spiritual and the sublime that He forgets the lowest needs of our nature. It is good to pass through these great ascriptions of praise to the simplicity of this lowly petition—*"Hallowed be Thy name. Thy kingdom come. Thy will be done in earth, as it is done in heaven."* It is as if I stood a little child and saw the great palace of the King of Kings in all its splendour, as if I stood amidst the ranks of Seraphim and Cherubim, all eager for their stately service; as if I looked forth over the kingdoms of the world and all the glory of them, and far away beyond I think of a million worlds through which His will has sway. What am I and my little common daily needs? But lo! the Almighty Father takes me by the hand and leads me into the banqueting chamber, and bids me look into His face and ask, *"Give me this day my daily bread."*

In the thought of the vastness of the universe we are apt to be lost, overwhelmed by its greatness, until it seems an impertinence to think that the Great Creator can concern Himself about creatures so insignificant on so minute a portion of His creation. Here, indeed, we cry with the Psalmist: *"When I consider Thy heavens, the work of Thy fingers, the sun and the moon which Thou hast ordained, what is man that Thou art mindful of him, or the son of man that Thou visitest him."*

"Look up at the sky at night; you will see a host of stars: try to think that every one of them is itself a sun. It may probably be that those suns have planets circulating round them, but it is hopeless for us to expect to see such planets. Were you standing on one of those stars and looking towards our system, you would not perceive the sun to be the brilliant and gorgeous object that we know so well. If you could see it at all, it would merely seem like a star, not nearly so bright as many of those you can see at night. Even if you had the biggest of telescopes to aid your vision, you could never discern from one of these bodies the planets which surround the sun. No astronomer in the stars could see Jupiter even if his sight were a thousand times as good or his telescope a thousand times as powerful as any sight or telescope that we know. So minute an object as our earth would, of course, be still more hopelessly beyond the possibility of vision." (Sir Robert Ball, *Starland.*)

Again we read another passage from the same writer, and are lost utterly in the sense of our insignificance.

"If the sun were to be extinguished altogether the calamity would no doubt be a very dire one so far as we are concerned, but the effect on the other celestial bodies (moon and planets excepted) would be of the slightest possible description. All the stars of heaven would continue to shine as before. Not a point in one of the constellations would be altered; not a variation in the brightness; not a change in the line of any star could be noticed. The thousands of nebulae and clusters would be absolutely unaltered. In fact, the total extinction of the sun would be hardly remarked in the newspapers published in the Pleiades or in Orion. There might possibly be a little line somewhere in an odd corner to the effect 'Mr. So-and-so, our well-known astronomer, has noticed that a tiny star, inconspicuous to the eye, and absolutely of no importance whatever, has now become invisible.'"

Amid such immensities what am I, or the common wants of a passing day!

Very blessed in the midst of such thoughts is it to turn to these words of the Lord Jesus. He leads us forth amidst the birds of the air that we may learn our greatness and dignity, and our claims as children of the Heavenly Father. *"Are ye not much better than they?"*

The tempter took the Lord Jesus up an exceeding high mountain and showed Him all the kingdoms of the world and the glory of them. Our Blessed Master leads us up the mountain height and shows us the gracious care of the Heavenly

Father to the least of His creatures that He may cure our worry.

It is as if He said, "Come, anxious child, and see the bounty of thy Heavenly Father; how that He openeth His hand and satisfieth the desire of every living thing." Every living thing—what a family is this to be provided for. Think if they could pass before us in all their variety and all their hosts. The myriad creatures that do inhabit the ocean; huge monsters each needing a vast supply. The shoals of fish that swim in millions, each with its separate need, increasing in number as they decrease in size, until we reach the tiny creatures whose universe is a drop of water—each with life to be sustained, each to be adapted to all the subtle influences on which its life depends.

Let us wander in the great forests and think of the creatures that roam within it. Shall we stand and let the procession pass before us—the stately monarchs of the woods; these that bound swift as the wind across the plains; these that crouch in their lurking places; these that find their strength in companies; these that people the trees; these that burrow in the earth? How vast the provision that is required.

Think again of the myriad hosts of the insect world, each with its need not only day by day, but hour by hour, and moment by moment, each with its very shape and instincts and powers perfectly adapted to its surroundings.

Let us behold the fowls of the air, again a mighty host—the eagle soaring in the height; the birds that fill the woods and valleys with their song; the great hosts of the sea-fowl. Think of their adaptation to their food, sometimes the plumage changing with the seasons for their safety. Think of the tender ingenuity that builds its nest so perfectly rounded and smoothed by the breast of the bird. Think of the mystery of their migration that brings these tiny hosts in millions unerringly across the mighty seas and under the trackless heavens for thousands of miles.

Then pass from the host of creatures to consider the least part of any of the most insignificant of these creatures. Is there anything, for instance, that seems of less concern than the dust from the wing of a moth or butterfly? Yet a French naturalist, M. Bernard Deschamps, tells us that each particle of dust is a scale composed of three membranes, or plates, laid one on the other. The first is covered with granulations of a moulded form, which give the thin scales their splendid and varied colouring. The second plate is covered with silk, forming sometimes various designs. The third plate, that which rests on the wing, has the peculiar property of reflecting colours the most brilliant and most varied. Suppose a painter were possessed of colours rich enough to represent on canvas, with all their splendour, gold, silver, the opal, the ruby, the sapphire, the emerald and other precious stones, one might affirm, without any fear of contradiction, that he would have no colour and no shade of colour which could not be discovered on part of the scales of a butterfly. Each of these scales is fastened to the wing by a small tube, and the scales are arranged in rows, each row partially overlapping the other.

Think again of the great provision which is needful to minister to all these hosts. Think of the forces of the mighty sun; the supplies of light and heat incessant; the adaptation of the seasons; the needful changes of day and night; the mystery of the air, ever renewed and waiting for the renewal of all life.

If our God can afford to keep so great a household, surely we need not fear. If our Father hath such a host of servants, His child shall certainly lack no good thing. These hired servants of our Father's have bread enough and to spare. Is God going to feed the great whales and the young lions and the ravens which cry, and forget thee? The hand that is opened to feed all these is stretched forth to grasp thy hand in love. So much for the servant, what then for the son? *"When he was yet a great way off his father saw him, and ran and fell on his neck, and kissed him. And he said, Bring forth the best robe and put it on him, and the ring for the finger, and the shoes for the feet.... And they began to be merry."*

Behold the fowls of the air. Are ye not much better than they? Therefore I say unto you, Be not anxious.

GOD IS NEAR THEE
Anonymous

❄

God is near thee, Christian cheer thee;
Rest in Him, sad soul;
He will keep thee, when around thee
Billows roll.

Calm thy sadness, look in gladness
To thy Friend on high;
Faint and weary pilgrim, cheer thee;
Help is nigh.

Mark the sea-bird wildly wheeling
Through the stormy skies;
God defends him, God attends him,
When he cries.

Fare thee onward, through the sunshine,
Or through wintry blast:
Fear forsake thee. God will take thee
Home at last.

CHAPTER **VI**

WHAT IS
the GOOD
of IT

*Which of you
by taking thought
can add one cubit
unto his stature?*

ST. MATTHEW 6:27

⊸⊨ What Is *the* Good *of* It ⊨⊷

HICH OF YOU BY BEING ANXIOUS CAN ADD ONE CUBIT *unto his stature?"*

Here is the next argument. Sit down and fret for a year and see how much bigger you are. You may well perhaps be something smaller; certainly shrivelled in soul if not in body—but you will be no bigger. Put the finger of one hand on the finger of the other and carry it down to your elbow, that is a cubit. Can you add that to your stature by your fretting and your care?

How quickly should we cease from worry if we did but think within ourselves—What good is it? Can you undo anything by fretting? Can you change it? Can you lessen it? If minding will not mend it, then better not to mind.

Some time ago I was talking with a friend of mine whom I had met in the train. I inquired after the health of his wife.

"Well," said he in reply, "my wife is well, always well, and always very well, and what is better still, she is always happy. I used to think that she had not the same sensitive nature that I have. When anything occurs to annoy me I am utterly upset. I cannot eat my breakfast; I cannot do my business; I am really ill. But the other day I found out the secret of my wife's complacency. Something had gone wrong which very much worried me. In the course of the morning I went into the house and found her cheerily going on with her work, actually singing as she bent over it; I felt quite annoyed.

"Really, my dear," I said, "you don't seem at all put out by what has happened today,"

"Oh, no," she said, "I am not."

"Well," I said, rather angrily, "then I think you ought to be."

"No, no, you must not say that. Look here. Years ago I made up my mind that when anything went wrong I would ask myself honestly and earnestly—'Can I do any good by thinking about it? Am I to blame in any way? If so, do not let me spare myself. Can I do anything to put a better face upon it?' If after looking at it honestly all round I found I could do no good, I made up my mind that I would give up thinking about it."

"Thank you," said I to my friend. "That is the philosophy of the highest life—'*Whatsoever things are lovely, think on these things.*'"

"But," said one to me one day, to whom I told this story, "I cannot help thinking about them."

"Then," said I, "you are the slave of the thing, and not the master. You remind me of a story I have heard of a soldier who on the field of battle called to his commanding officer, 'Captain, I have got a prisoner.' 'Bring him on then, my man,' said the captain. 'Please, sir, he won't come,' was the answer. 'Then come yourself,' cried the captain. 'Please, sir, he won't let me.'"

We ask often how much a man possesses. That is not the question. The question is how much possesses him.

Some time ago I was at the house of a gentleman in Yorkshire, who said to me, "I used to be a most irritable man. When anything went wrong I fussed and fumed, was miserable myself, and made all about me miserable. My religious influence was worse than undone. I suffered in health and I suffered in my business. But one day I pulled myself up and said, 'Look here, you are a fool!'"

Whilst we are forbidden to call our brother a fool, it is well to hurl the epithet at ourselves if we deserve it.

"You are a fool," I said to myself. "If your religion does not cure your temper, what has it done for you?" I made up my mind that I would bring all the strength of my will and all the grace of God that I could get to bear upon this besetment. Now I do not want to boast, but I thank God that it is a very long time since I found myself fretting or worried. I cannot tell you the difference it makes, not only to myself in the happiness of my own life, but in the happiness of those about me.

Here is a homely counsel on worry which we may take to heart.

DON'T YOU TROUBLE TROUBLE
Anonymous

Within a garden by the cottage door
Sits an old mother, knitting busily,
Hair snowy white beneath a snow-white cap;
Eyes blue as the blue skies that arch the place;
A face all full of peace and sunny hopes.
A cheery song she sings, a moment stayed
To count the stitches and to set them right
Then click the needles music to her song.
From her I learned this counsel upon care:

Don't you trouble trouble
Till trouble troubles you.
Don't you look for trouble;
Let trouble look for you.

Don't you borrow sorrow;
You'll surely have your share.
He who dreams of sorrow
Will find that sorrow's there.

Don't you hurry worry
By worrying lest it come.
To flurry is to worry,
'Twill miss you if you're mum.

If care you've got to carry;
Wait till 'tis at the door,
For he who runs to meet it
Takes up the load before.

If minding will not mend it,
Then better not to mind;
The best thing is to end it
Just leave it all behind.

Who feareth hath forsaken
The Heavenly Father's side;
What He hath undertaken
He surely will provide.

The very birds reprove thee
With all their happy song:
The very flowers teach thee
That fretting is a wrong.

"Cheer up," the sparrow chirpeth,
"Thy Father feedeth me;
Think how much more He careth,
Oh, lonely child, for thee."

"Fear not," the flowers whisper,
"Since thus He hath arrayed
The buttercup and daisy,
How canst thou be afraid?"

Then don't you trouble trouble,
Till trouble troubles you;
You'll only double trouble,
And trouble others too.

CHAPTER VII

CONSIDER
the LILIES

*Wherefore, if God so
clothe the grass of the
field... shall He not
much more clothe you?*

ST. MATTHEW 6:30

✠ Consider *the* Lilies ✠

HERE IS AN EXQUISITE BIT OF TENDERNESS IN THE story of the Creation that it will do us good to notice. Of all the vast heaven and earth we read God spake and it was done. He said, *"Let there be light, and there was light."* At the bidding of His word there came the grass and trees, and the herb-yielding seed. At His command there came the creatures that flew in the heavens, or filled the seas, or roamed on the land. But when God comes to deal with man and with flowers there is a new method. The Lord God formed man, and breathed into his nostrils the breath of life, and the man became a living soul. And the Lord God planted a garden, and there He put the man whom He had formed. The flowers come in with the man; the man with the flowers. Geology shows us that in the earlier ages there grew vast reeds and tree-ferns, but no flowers.

And the garden was the first sanctuary. There amid the flowers that spake the "fear not" of God to the heart of man, and that proclaimed His gracious care, He walked and talked with His child. And there in the garden was such pure worship as no stately cathedral has ever known.

And when the Lord Jesus comes to restore our Paradise and to teach us of the Father, He does not gather His disciples about Him in the temple. He goes there indeed, but it is sternly to reprove, indignantly to overthrow the tables of the money-changers—to drive forth the sheep and oxen with their defilement, and to scatter the seats of those that sold doves. But when He would open His mouth and teach His disciples, He went up into the mountain, and sat down amidst the abundance of flowers. We must not picture the scene like that of our own mountain slopes, beautiful as they may be with purple heather and golden furze, and daisies bright and shining buttercups. Palestine is the land of flowers. Its most striking feature is the abundance of flowers, their variety and brilliance. A land flowing with milk and honey meant, in other words, a land of rich pastures and many flowers. "A Garden of Eden run wild," says Canon Tristram. So we must think of the mountain slope where the Great Teacher sits as rainbow-hued with flowers. And here, as in the garden that the Lord God planted of old, the Saviour finds the sanctuary, and picking a flower He held it up and said: *"Consider the lilies of the field, how they grow."*

"Consider the lilies of the field." There is much in that. The flowers that are wholly and only dependent on the Father's care. Not the garden flowers that have a man trained in all knowledge of flower lore to take care of them. Nor the hot-house flowers screened from the sun and sheltered from the frost with all kinds of costly appliance for their culture. The lilies of the field, the trembling buttercup and daisy that the wind can wither and the frost can kill, that the sheep can nib-ble and the oxen trample—these are to bring us the sweet mes-sage of the Heavenly Father's care.

"Consider the lilies." It is the bidding of the Blessed Lord. He would have us not only look at them, not only admire them, not only think about them. It is rather, Be still and let them preach to you. Let us seek from Him the anointed eye, the opened ear, the tuned heart.

Look at it, the beauty of the shape, the richness of the col-our, the powdered gold, the grace of stem, the tender care of swathing leaves about the bud. The very seasons are set, and the sun shines and the showers fall, and the mysterious ener-gies of the earth are controlled for the flower's sake. These all wait upon the flower and minister to it. All the forces of Nature are charged concerning the flower.

If God cares so much for flowers He must be very kind and patient and gentle. What images and thoughts of God the world had in the old time, and what thoughts some men have still. They listened to the thunder and said it was His voice;

they saw the lightning flash and said that God passed by. When the mountain flamed and melted, the people fled, crying: *"Let not God speak with us lest we die."* The prophet sought for Him in the fire that fused the solid rock and ran along the ground; and in the whirlwind that swept and roared resistless in its might; and in the earthquake that shook the solid hills. But lo! He cometh who hath seen the Father, and He saith: "Consider the lilies of the field. Behold the fowls of the air. Your Heavenly Father careth much more for you."

I have known men who did not care for flowers. They have been so taken up with business that their hearts have become asphalted, as hard and barren as the city streets, trodden by the restless feet of a thousand fretting thoughts, and where the heavy waggons of their worries go rumbling all the day and far into the night. They have no room for what they call sentiment. The children are troublesome and are banished into the nursery; the birds are noisy and should be shot; and as for the flower-garden, they would turn it into a potato ground, unless flowers pay better—then they like flowers. Now I might go to such people for advice; they know all the good investments; they are sharp, shrewd, what the world calls clever. But I should never dream of going to them for sympathy, for pity, for help. I hold the flower in my hand and I feel at once how gracious He must be who makes the flowers—how pitiful, how patient, how tender, with what care and skill He deals with things. These are the proof and pledge of

His tenderness. *"If God so clothe the grass of the field—the common flower of the hedgerow and the pasture—shall He not much more clothe you?"*

Consider the lilies, and see how He delights to give. In poor-houses and prisons—alas! that we should have to put them together, and that poverty should be treated so much as if it were a crime—the food is allowanced, the weight exact, lest a bit too much should be given—bread to the crumb and rice to the grain. They may claim enough for bare existence, but must not ask for more. Even kindness and pity find their limits in men's wants. They look up what they can spare, and give their scraps and cast-offs. But love, glad love, cannot bear to weigh and measure. Love cannot limit itself to wants and stop there. Love must give its luxuries. Love must lavish its best, its all. *"Bring out the best robe, the ring for the finger, the shoes for the feet"*—all these are luxuries, not necessaries, in Palestine—*"and bring hither the fatted calf"*—the daintiest and best. Flowers are the overflow of God's love, the luxuries thrown in. It is much that He should give us bread to eat, and water to drink, and light to see by, and air to breathe; but these cannot satisfy Him—His love must go farther, and He sends us the flowers and bids them bring the assurance, "Your Heavenly Father careth for you."

Consider the lilies, and see again how God loves beauty. Our Heavenly Father cares for the look, the shape, the colour of things. He decks the heavens with glory, and makes the flowers beautiful. *"Shall He not much more clothe you?"* Is there not more in the word than we sometimes think? It certainly means that God will give the needful clothing; but does it not mean more than that? Shall He not deck and adorn His children? Shall He not array them in beauty if He so clothe the grass of the field, which today is and tomorrow is gone? The beauty of the Lord our God is to be upon us. He who teaches the birds their song, how it must grieve Him when His children speak harsh, angry, unkind words. He who makes the daisy and peeping violet so beautiful, how it must hurt Him when His children are hideous with envy, ugly with pride, scarred by meanness and selfishness. What a blot and stain upon His fair creation!

Consider the lilies and see how God makes His beauty. What a complicated process it is when man manufactures his beautiful things. The axe must cut down; the tree must be rent; the plane must smooth; the turning lathe and chisel must be at work; dust fills the air; chips and shavings litter the ground. There is the din of the hammer and the heat of the fire. I watched one making his flowers of glass—here the fierce furnace, heated to its uttermost; then the lump of glass thrust into the glare, twisted and turned; then the pincers seizing it and pulling it and pushing it, and then the thing plunged into the fire again and again. I turned away and thought within myself—Some people think that is how God makes us beautiful.

Consider the lilies how they grow—grow: furnace and heat, hacking and hewing, rending and tearing—hammer and pincers—where are they? Tell us, lily, how did He make thee beautiful? "Oh, He blew me about with His south wind, and sent His great sun to shine upon me, and refreshed me with the showers, and the dew came noiselessly while I slept. Day after day He cared for me, and I came to this." Do not be afraid of the processes of God in beautifying us. He does not burn and beat and break that we may be adorned; but He breathes His south wind, and shines upon us with His favour, and shapes us by His grace, and so He makes us beautiful.

Again, *"Consider the lilies how they grow."* Here is the balance of earth and heaven—the ministry of each accepted; the claims of each satisfied. Here heaven and earth do meet and blend. The dark root lay in the ground, down amongst the clods of the earth, and on the stick that marked the place was thrust a label with a name grand enough to turn the head of any simple flower. And the lily said: "What have I to do in this dirty earth? Faugh! I cannot bear to touch it. I, who belong to the *Lilia Splendiosa*, to be prisoned here like this! I know my place too well to think that I was meant for such a dungeon—cold, damp, dark—as if indeed I were dead and buried. I ought to be up in the heavens, lifting my head proudly, and unfolding all my glory to the sun." And it sulked, and muttered, and refused to thrust out the root. So it missed heaven because it neglected earth.

Take care how you grumble at your circumstances—so many difficulties, so many hindrances to cry out against. To do our duty on earth is the only way of getting to heaven.

But think of another flower that should say, "Oh! it is all a mistake to call me a lily. Lily indeed! I am just a poor dirty brown thing, and haven't any beauty in me. Without any stem, without any leaf, it is no use my dreaming of heaven and hoping to be anything." And it thrust down its roots into the earth, but it forgot to push its stem up into the light!

The heavenly-minded man who neglects his duty in the world is as unlovely to God as he is ugly to men. And the man that is so absorbed in earth that he forgets heaven misses the very beauty and blessedness of life.

The message of the flowers ends with this much more. The Maker of the flowers is our Heavenly Father. God's delight in His works prompts the perfection of their beauty. But love needs more than the flowers can bring. Love seeketh not its own, yet love ever seeketh itself. Love only finds love, and love only loves love. That we are made in the likeness and image of God, the one creature in all the world that is capable of knowing Him—that to us is spoken the command to love Him with all the heart—means that we are infinitely more and dearer to Him than any other creature can be. Much more; that infinitely more is ours. Lift your eyes from the lily of the field to Him who holds it in His hand. For the lily God hath given the sunshine and shower, and the orderly seasons and the refreshing dew, but for us He hath sent the Blessed Lord Himself, the Well-beloved. And turn again from the lily in its beauty and fragrance to Him, and think how He is going on to the darkness and agony of the Cross—giving Himself for us *"that He may present us to Himself, a glorious Church, not having spot or wrinkle or any such thing."* If the beauty of the flower be the outcome of the sunshine and shower, what finished beauty, what perfect blessedness is that which shall satisfy Him, who hath loved us and given Himself for us.

"Solomon in all his glory was not arrayed like one of these." It is not only that the beauty of the flower outpasses the glory of Solomon, but the method of that beauty. The glory of Solomon was all "put on"—the glory of the flower is all "wrought out."

King Solomon would have a crown of the finest of gold, but he could not make it. He must send for Hiram, the widow's son. And I think the man who can make a crown and make it well may be more royal than the man who can only wear it when someone else makes it. Solomon would have some royal robes, splendid robes wrought with the finest of needlework, but he could not make them. The women must make them, and they who made them did a more noble thing than he who only wore them. She whom this generation will think of as our Queen, Victoria the Beloved, would never have been what she is today in the hearts of her people because of the crown upon her head and the robes about her shoulders. It was the queenliness from within, not from without, that made her glory and her greatness. God makes His kings not by trappings from without, but unfoldings from within. You must grow the true glory like the flowers—you cannot put it on.

LESSONS FROM THE FLOWERS
Anonymous

✽

Flowers preach to us if we will hear—
The rose saith in the dewy morn:
I am most fair;
Yet all my loveliness is born
Upon a thorn.
The poppy saith amid the corn:
Let but my scarlet head appear
And I am held in scorn;
Yet juice of subtle virtue lies
Within my cup of curious dyes.
The lilies say: Behold how we
Preach without words of purity.
The violets whisper from the shade
Which their own leaves have made:
Men scent our fragrance on the air,
Yet take no heed

Of humble lessons we would read.
But not alone the fairest flowers:
The merest grass
Along the roadside where we pass,
Lichen and moss and sturdy weed,
Tell of His love who sends the dew,
The rain and sunshine too
To nourish one small seed.

CHAPTER VIII

The

HEATHENISM

of WORRY

*After all these things
do the Gentiles seek.*

ST. MATTHEW 6:32

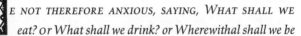

The Heathenism *of* Worry

E NOT THEREFORE ANXIOUS, SAYING, WHAT SHALL WE
eat? or What shall we drink? or Wherewithal shall we be
clothed? For after all these things do the Gentiles seek: for your
Heavenly Father knoweth that ye have need of all these things. But seek
ye first His kingdom, and His righteousness; and all these things shall
be added unto you. Be not therefore anxious for the morrow, for the morrow will be anxious for itself. Sufficient unto the day is the evil thereof."

Here is the next argument: The heathenism of worry.
"After these things do the heathen seek," those who never heard
of the Father's love, who never knew of the tender care of
our God.

This heathenism of worry is a double wrong; it is a forgetfulness of God and a degradation of life; all is absorbed in eat-
ing and drinking, bent downward over the husks and blind to
the heavens, deaf to the voices that call us up higher.

93

These two aspects of worry are met by the two remaining counsels. For the first, the remedy is in the assurance, *"Your Heavenly Father knoweth that ye have need of all these things."*

For the second comes the command, *"Seek ye first His kingdom and His righteousness and all these things shall be added unto you."*

To look down, and only down, with fear and anxiety is the life of the heathen.

To look up to the Father's love and then to look down, is to find a confidence in which fear and worry are lost.

This is ever the difference between the land of the heathen and the home of the children of God. Egypt is the land where they look down for everything. The rising of the Nile brought the supply of all wants, whilst Canaan is the land that drinketh in the rain of the water of Heaven. Between the two lay the school of the wilderness, where Israel was trained in this art of looking up; down from Heaven came their daily bread. Their shade, their guidance, their protection, their all was in Heaven above. Only when they had learned to look up were they ready rightly to look down upon the land that flowed with milk and honey.

After these things *do the heathen seek.* He who frets has lost his God—is indeed as if God were not.

Surely it is worse than having no God, to kneel down and say, *"Our Father who art in Heaven,"* and then to go forth fretting and fearing as if He never knew or cared.

It is worse than being an orphan to have a Father and yet forget His love.

How perplexed the angels must be at the sight of the fretting child of a Heavenly Father.

"Has he not a Father?" asks one in amazement. "Does not his Father love him?" says another. "Does not his Father know all about him?" says a third. "Is not his Father great and rich?" asks a fourth. "Has not his Father given us charge concerning him?" say they all. "How then can he fret?"

If there be one grain of truth in our belief that there is a living God who holds us unutterably dear, who is seeking in all things and through all things ever to lead us to the highest, the fullest, to the best, what room is there for us to fret or fear?

"Your Heavenly Father knoweth that ye have need of all these things." Some time ago I was reading a book on "Geology" by Professor Geikie. I came across a statement that arrested me and filled me with wonder. "It is calculated that the river Rhine brings down annually lime enough to supply three hundred and thirty-three million oysters with shells."

It was during my holidays, and I was fishing off the coast of Guernsey. I read it to the boatmen who were with me, and it was the topic for a day's conversation. I saw in my mind the Alps rise mighty and majestic holding communion with the stars. What to them with their heads in Heaven could be the little paltry things of the far-off sea? And yet from these must come the lime for oyster shells.

I saw the sun in the heavens lighting up the worlds, so far away with its exhaustless energies of light and heat. What to it were the needs of tiny hidden things in the ocean's depth? And yet the sun was lifting up the vapours into the heights where they became snow; and the snow in turn became the glacier that ground and ground the mountains into lime for oyster shells.

I saw ten thousand leaping, laughing water-falls flinging themselves from the heights, eager, ceaseless, resistless, as if they knew the glad errand on which they went, bringing down the supply for the tiny creatures that waited in the North Sea. And then I saw the stately river Rhine, proud arbiter of nations, flowing past the cities that it made great, and underneath the shadow of ancient castles that it had made safe, and it hastened on its way bearing the material in which the oysters were to find their shells.

My heart laughed within me with the glad faith—What a thing it is to be an oyster! And yet are we not much better than they? *"Your Heavenly Father knoweth that ye have need of all these things."*

Look back and see the marvellous provision that the Heavenly Father has made for every one of us. There was a time when we were all want and nothing but want. If we could have anticipated our coming into this world no dream of horror could ever have seemed so dreadful.

If we could have stood and said, "I am going into that strange world, the most helpless thing in it. Of course I shall know nobody, and of course no one will know me. I shall not be able to understand their language, and I shall not have the sense to know my own wants, much less to tell them to any one else. I shall be so little that of course no one will care for me, I shall be in everybody's way and quite unable to get out of it." Oh, the agony of it, that cruel loneliness. The angels surely shuddered the first time they saw a baby, and wondered that God dared make anything so awful in its helplessness.

No terror that ever came into a man's mind in thought of going out of this world would have compared with that terror of coming into it.

And lo! we came—and a mother's love bent over us. Oh, the marvellous and perfect ministry. Little—and yet because little so unutterably dear. Weak—yes, omnipotently weak. Waited upon day and night with a service unwearied, a service that found its Heaven in its ministry. The power that made a mother is the power that I can trust for ever and ever. A mother is the "Fear not" of nature to our hearts.

Now may we think of our gracious God speaking to us, "Come let us reason together, My child. There was a time when thou wert all want, and in that time didst thou lack anything? Was not every want anticipated and perfectly supplied? And the love that fashioned the mother for thee at the beginning of thy life is the love that still holds thee dear, caring as surely and sacredly for the wants of manhood and of old age as for the wants of the little child."

"Your Heavenly Father knoweth that ye have need of all these things."

But seek ye first His kingdom and His righteousness.

So we reach again the great lesson that the Gospel of Jesus Christ is a power within us to keep the man right with things.

All the money in the world will not hurt a man if he keeps it in the right place, but two brass farthings will blind him if he puts them over his eyes. We are wrong with things, little or great, when they hide from us the vision of the heavenly; when they deafen us to the voices that are ever calling us higher; when they deaden us to the impulses and promptings of the Good Spirit; when they divert us from the path in which God would lead us.

"All these things shall be added unto you." Note well how much. God never promises to make a rich man. I am glad of that, though I should not mind trying the experiment. There is an awful law that runs through all things, which finds its cruellest force in money. The more a man has the less he thinks he has. All that God promises is all that we need, not all that we desire. Our desires are infinite—they are made for God, and what is great enough for Him is too great for anything less.

We are always trying to make ourselves little enough for the world to fill us, and we cannot. This is the source of our divine discontent. We perish with hunger so long as we seek to fill ourselves with the husks the swine do eat. It is only in the Father's house that there is bread enough and to spare, and the heart will never be merry with the abiding merriment until we arise and go to the Father.

All these things—how much? As much as God gives the birds, and as much as He gives the flowers; and think how much that is. For the birds, a nest to lie in and a heaven to fly in. Come, if I have that I am well off. A nest to lie in and a heaven to fly in.

As much as He gives the flowers: and how much is that? Earth to grow in, and Heaven to go into. If I have that, then how much more do I want?

Somebody said to me one day, "I suppose you have not much of the garden living in London?"

"Well," I said, "it depends which way you measure it. It is many miles deep and many miles high and about six feet across." That is what God gives us all. Plenty of depth, plenty of height and as much across as we can stand on, and if we had more we could not be in two places at once.

Therefore I say unto you, Be not anxious.

⋅⋅⋅ ⊷⊹⊷ ⋅⋅⋅

The weight that a man carries upon his back is altogether determined by the size of the world beneath his feet. In those lectures in which Sir Robert Ball has put the mystery of the heavens within the compass of such simple and unskilled folks as most of us are, he says that a man who carries a sack of corn on earth could as easily carry six sacks of corn on a globe the size of the moon. But in a world as vast as the sun even to pull out the watch from the pocket would be to tug at a weight of some five or six pounds, and that it would be impossible, indeed, to lift the arm; and if once a man were to lie down there he could never get up again.

That is the truth, the very truth, we have to learn. Our burdens are heavy, not in themselves but in the attraction and gravitation of the earth. If the earth is all to us, then, alas! how true is it that its burdens crush and overwhelm us, and then indeed we can scarcely lift a hand to heaven, all unable to raise ourselves to higher things. The Lord Jesus Christ has come to bring in our midst the forces of another Kingdom that are able to loosen and lessen the attraction of the earth. Above us and about us, hidden and unheard, but ever present, ever mighty, is the power of the Kingdom of God and His Righteousness. So is it that for us the yoke of life is made easy, the burden of life is made light, and we enter into rest.

Nor is this all. The truth is made complete by yet another illustration from astronomy. The last of the planets was discovered by no telescopic observation, but by mathematical calculations. It was found to be attracted from its ordinary and regular course by some strange and unknown body, whose exact position was determined by means of these calculations. This is the fulness of the blessed truth. The gentle yet mighty forces of another world are brought into this by the Lord Jesus Christ, forces that attract and draw us to Himself. *"I have overcome the world,"* saith He. So are we set in our true position toward earth and heaven. The burden gone, it is easy to live like the lark of which Wordsworth sings.

TO SOAR, YET NOT TO ROAM
Anonymous

❀

"To soar, yet not to roam,
True to the kindred points of heaven and home."
O Lord, how happy should we be
If we could cast our care on Thee,
If we from self could rest;
And feel at heart that One above,
In perfect wisdom, perfect love,
Is working for the best.

Could we but kneel, and cast our load,
E'en while we pray, upon our God,
Then rise with lightened cheer;
Sure that the Father, Who is nigh
To still the famished raven's cry,
Will hear in that we fear.

Lord, make these faithless hearts of ours
Such lessons learn from birds and flowers;
Make them from self to cease,
Leave all things to a Father's will,
And find, before Him lying still,
E'en in affliction, peace.

CHAPTER IX

An
APOSTOLIC
INJUNCTION

*Casting all your care upon
Him for He careth for you.*

1 ST. PETER 5:7

⊱ *An* Apostolic Injunction ⊰

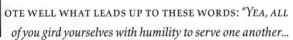OTE WELL WHAT LEADS UP TO THESE WORDS: *"YEA, ALL of you gird yourselves with humility to serve one another... Humble yourselves therefore under the mighty hand of God, casting all your anxiety upon Him because He careth for you."*

The greater half of our worries, certainly the most irritating half, comes from our pride. Worry hath many wives, but I think Conceit hath borne him the most children, and these the most greedy and unruly of them all. To humble ourselves is to be rid of many of our heaviest burdens. It is well for us to set as frontispiece the picture on which St. Peter is looking as he writes these words. We find the clue to the scene in this phrase: *"Be clothed with humility."* The word is used nowhere else in the Bible. It refers to the apron of coarse texture which was worn by the slave when he made himself ready for service.

It was the mark of his subjection. So we may read it, Be towelled with humility.

The Word at once takes us back to the scene of the Last Supper. There starts before us that incident which would remain for ever vivid in the minds of the disciples, and most of all in the case of Peter. The guest chamber had been made ready for the Master and His disciples. The good-man of the house had set the water in the room and made all provision for the feast, and then had withdrawn. Now the disciples begin to take their places at the table. It was probably the only occasion in which they had sat at such a ceremonious gathering, and it may be that the dispute which broke out amongst them was caused by the very order of their sitting.

The Supper is ended, and there beneath the very shadow of the Cross, the sacred emblems of the Holy Sacrament before their very eyes, they argue angrily as to which of them shall be the greatest. The dispute seems to have been referred to the Lord Himself for His decision. Eagerly they wait for the word which should settle the matter once for all. Very solemn, very impressive is the reply of the Master. Not in words that they could forget, but in a scene to be for ever graven upon their memories, is the answer given. In that silence they watch Him rise from the couch on which He reclined. He begins to take off His outer garments and lay them aside—no stately robe was it, but the simple vesture of the peasant woven from top to bottom. Then, taking the towel, He girds Himself as the slave, thrusting the corner of it beneath the fold at His side. Eagerly their eyes follow Him as He passes to the pitcher and lifts it and pours the water into a basin. Then, setting it down beside one of the disciples, most likely Peter, He begins to wash his feet. Peter is shamed and troubled by such condescension, and shrinking from those outstretched hands, he cried almost reprovingly, *"Thou shalt never wash my feet."*

"If I wash thee not, thou hast no part in Me," was the Lord's reply.

Then all the soul bursts forth in entreaty, *"Lord, not my feet only, but my hands and my head."*

So knelt their Lord before each of them in turn. The work done, He rose and again put on His garments and sat down in their midst. *"Know ye what I have done?"* He asked. *"Ye call Me Lord and Master and ye say well, for so I am. I have given you an example that ye should do as I have done with you."*

The scene comes back to Peter now in all its vividness, that consuming worry of each for his own importance that provoked the unseemly dispute. And, moved by that sad memory, he writes: *"Yea, all of you gird yourselves with humility to serve one another...Humble yourselves under the mighty hand of God...Casting all your anxiety upon Him because He careth for you."*

He who is ever seeking to assert his own importance, greedy for the recognition of his greatness, lives in a perpetual worry. Pride, however much it has, claims ever more. We may say of pride what Matthew Henry says of sin: "Nature is satisfied with little, grace with less, pride with nothing." He who puts on the towel of service, puts off a world of worry. There is no surer and no readier remedy for our own worries than to try and lessen the worries of other people. When the little pin-pricks of life's annoyances rankle and fester, it is a symptom of too much self-indulgence and too little exercise. Mr. Wesley tells how that once, sitting beside some rich man in his drawing-room, there came down a puff of smoke from the chimney. "Ah, Mr. Wesley," sighed the rich man, "these are the annoyances which I have to endure." Poor rich man, how he would have lost his annoyances if he had measured them by the annoyances of most other people. He who seeks to bring a ray of sunshine to some soul, and a song within some heart, shall himself walk beneath blue skies, and his feet shall move to strains of heavenly music.

"Casting all your care upon Him for He careth for you," so the old version has it, but the two words rendered care are very different. The care which we are to cast upon the Lord is the distraction, the worry, the anxiety against which the Lord Jesus warns us, but the care of God is in taking care of us. We are to lose our worry in being taken care of. This word, too, was used by the Lord Jesus, and it is well to recall its association. When the Good Samaritan brings the man to the inn, whom he found in the way, wounded and stripped, he directs them to take care of him, to see that he wants nothing. So it is that we, beaten and burdened by a crowd of cruel fears and anxieties,

are to find our refuge under God's Almighty Hand, and to find our rest in His care.

We in our pride are apt to think that to humble ourselves is to be forced to an unwilling surrender, a hard necessity of submission. But with our gracious Father, to humble is not to humiliate. The true and best humility is that which love wins from us as the sunshine and soft breath of spring woo the flowers from the hedgerow. Of old, when God would humble Israel, He fed them with angels' food, or as it is rendered in the margin, *"Everyone did eat the bread of the mighty"* (Ps. 78:25).

God loves us into humility.

To humble ourselves under the mighty hand of God is to live in happy submission to His will, in restful assurance that over all and through all and in all there is at work for us the love which can only be satisfied with that which makes for our highest, fullest, richest good. *"Thy will be done"* is not a sigh of compulsion, but a triumphant song.

> *Brave trust in God be thine alway,*
> *So shalt thou rest*
> *Infallible; if day by day*
> *He have in all things His own way,*
> *Thou shalt be blest:*
> *And good shall be yet more than good—*
> *God's very best.*

To humble ourselves under God's mighty hand is to find the fulfilment of the promise made to Benjamin, of all the promises made to Israel surely the sweetest and best. *"The beloved of the Lord shall dwell in safety by Him: And the Lord shall cover him all the day long."* In such a dwelling place, compassed with that favour as with a shield, instinctively, almost of necessity, we cast all our care upon Him who careth so graciously for us.

"Casting all your anxiety upon the Lord, because He careth for you." Is it not the deepest bitterest cry of many a heart—Nobody cares for me? There are hosts of men and women ready to give in, who could go bravely on in life's wind and rain, if somewhere a little bit of love awaited for them to keep the heart warm—some old mother to speak the name tenderly and bless it as she spoke, or some little child to brighten at their coming.

> *"If the veriest cur would lick my hand,*
> *I could love it like a child."*

We have heard of worry killing its hosts; but there is something more cruel than that. Untended, unmourned, unmoved, men die because they find no one to care for them. Here is the great and blessed cure for worry. The Lord careth for you.

Therefore cast all your worry upon Him. Many can cast the burden of their sins upon the Lord who yet do carry the burden of their daily worries.

One hot summer day I was driving along when I overtook a woman who carried a heavy basket. She gladly accepted my offer of a ride, but sat with the heavy basket still on her arm.

"My good woman," I said. "Your basket will ride just as well in the bottom of the carriage and you would be much more comfortable,"

"So it would, sir, thank you," said she. "I never thought of that."

"That is what I do very often, too," I said.

The woman looked up inquiringly. "Yes, I do the same thing. The Lord Jesus has taken me up in His chariot and I rejoice to ride in it. But very often I carry a burden of worry on my back that would ride just as well if I put it down. If the Lord is willing to carry me, He is willing to carry my worries."

Cast your worry. It is not enough to put it down while we pray, and then shouldering it once more to go groaning up the hill. It is to have done with it—to fling it right away—fling it off and let it sink down in the ocean of God's great love.

The Lord careth for you. In that touching story of the mother who hid her little son for three months after the king's decree that the male children should be slain, what a picture is there of troubled worry. What terribly wearying months they were. How the mother smothered the little one's cry lest her secret be betrayed. How often she started and listened with beating heart at the sound of the passing footsteps. How in her dreams she saw that dreadful end, and woke stretching eager hands to assure herself of the child's safety.

But today the king's daughter has found the child and has compassion upon it. The king's daughter has taken the little one to her arms, and has said: "He shall be my son."

Now how safe is the little one, the son of Pharaoh's daughter. Every soldier grasped the glittering weapon to defend her child. All the wealth of Egypt ministered to his wants. All the might of Pharaoh girt him about with honour and safety. For him nothing was too much to ask or claim. The mother's worry is gone now—flung to the winds. Her child is called the son of Pharaoh's daughter.

The Lord careth for you. Cast off your burden of worry in the safety of His care. All that He is and has is yours for your safety and welfare. *Behold what manner of love the Father has bestowed on us that we might be called the children of God*—and such we are.

A SAFE STRONGHOLD OUR GOD IS

Martin Luther, 1529
Translated from German by Thomas Carlyle

A safe stronghold our God is still,
A trusty shield and weapon;
He'll help us clear from all the ill
That hath us now o'ertaken.
The ancient prince of hell
Hath risen with purpose fell;
Strong mail of craft and power
He weareth in this hour;
On earth is not his fellow.

With force of arms we nothing can,
Full soon were we down-ridden;
But for us fights the proper Man,
Whom God Himself hath bidden.
Ask ye who is this same?
Christ Jesus is His name,
Of Sabbaoth the Lord,
Sole God to be adored,
'Tis He must win the battle.

And were this world all devils o'er,
And watching to devour us,
We lay it not to heart to sore;
Not they can overpower us.
And let the prince of ill
Look grim as e'er he will,
He harms us not a whit;
For why? his doom is writ;
A word shall quickly slay him.

God's word, for all their craft and force,
One moment will not linger,
But, spite of hell, shall have its course;
'Tis written by His finger.
And, though they take our life,
Goods, honour, children, wife,
Yet is their profit small;
These things shall vanish all,
The city of God remaineth.

CHAPTER X

The
CROWN
and CLIMAX
of IT ALL

Who shall separate us
from the love of Christ?

ROMANS 8:35

"Who shall separate us from the love of Christ?"

"Nay, in all these things we are more than conquerors through Him that loved us. For I am persuaded that neither death, nor life, nor angels, nor principalities, nor things present, nor things to come, nor powers, nor height, nor depth, nor any other creature, shall be able to separate us from the love of God which is in Christ Jesus our Lord."

⟞ *The* CROWN *and* CLIMAX *of* IT ALL ⟝

CHAPTER X

HERE ARE THINGS TOO GREAT FOR THE LORD JESUS Christ to utter; our words are too shallow to hold them.

Let us come again and sit beside the Master on the mountain top, and looking into His face, let us ask, "Whence hath He come, the glorious Son of God?"

Think how for us men and for our salvation He has come down from His high estate to be the Babe of Bethlehem, to dwell amid the rough conditions of our daily life, to toil as we must toil and share with us earth's common wants.

Let us look into His face again and ask, Whither doth He go? Think how for us men and for our salvation He goes on to all the shame and agony of His most dreadful Cross. Then let the words sink down into the innermost heart. He that spared not His own Son, but delivered Him up for us all, how shall He not also with Him freely give us all things? That is the measure of the Heavenly Father's love and the pledge of our supply. The love that gave the Well-beloved is no past love. The Cross of Christ is not the high mark of a great love that once swept and surged about the world. It is the measure of the abiding love that ever holds us dear, the love that concerns itself about our every little worry and counts the common want a sacred thing to which He hath a joy in ministering, like the joy of a mother in ministering to her child.

For the cure of worry the Son of God reveals the love of the Heavenly Father and for our deliverance from this ill as from the deliverance of every ill, here is the fullest revelation of the Father's love in the gift of the well-beloved Son. Let us seek to rise step by step towards the fulness and height of these great words, praying that we may find in them that triumph in which the Apostle exults so rapturously.

Who shall separate us from the love of Christ? But is there not another question; what oneness can there be between Him and us. God and man?—The King of Saints and the chief of sinners—What can ever make them one? Between the glorious Son of God and us there must yawn the gulf of an infinite distance.

That His love may bind us into oneness with Himself, think of the Son of God becoming man in all points as we are. To make the lowest and the least of us one with Himself He lays aside His glory and becomes the lowly brother of us all;

He who was rich becomes poor for our sakes, and makes Himself one with us in the lowly surroundings of His life.

But yet remains that deepest gulf which severs us. We have sinned. Is there not a kind of dreadful comfort in shrinking from the sight of those eyes that look us through, and see as we have never seen our own vanity, our faults, our folly, and our sin? We cry as Peter cried in that too glorious presence: "Depart from me, O Lord, for I am a sinful man." Yet even here the Saviour meets us in a mystery of oneness. He bare our sins in His own body on the tree. He gives Himself to die for us, the Just for the unjust, that He might bring us to God. Dwell upon it all, the height from which He came, the depth to which He sank, the great things He hath wrought. Herein is love. With Him all things also must assuredly be ours.

He who can make these words his own, resting as sure of them as of the groundwork beneath his feet, lives evermore the conqueror in all things and of all things.

Let us be bold to claim them as our own. The Cross of Christ is the glorious revelation of God's love to the world, but it is more than that only; it focusses the infinite love and throws it burning and transforming upon the heart that bows beneath it. It is ours and all our own. The love that endured disgrace and poverty and pain could only be for such as we are. Now is it ours to ask this question with a boldness triumphant as his of old, *"Who shall separate us from the love of Christ?"*

Let us find in this love all that the Apostle did, seeing it is ours as it was his. He rose up in it ever strong for victory, ready for any condition and any circumstances. He challenged and defied all forces that could oppose him as he felt the glowing love of Christ within the soul. He put that love as if to every possible test, and in it found himself ever triumphant. See this man as he stands and looks forth upon his foes. Surely never was man faced by so threatening and terrible a host. There is Tribulation, a giant stained with blood, the flail upon his shoulder, threshing men and women as the thresher threshes corn. There is Distress stripping life of all that gladdens it. There is Persecution, leading on his accursed crew, prison, torture, outrage, agony. There is Famine, gaunt and hollow-eyed, blighting with her breath and bringing in her train a hundred forms of ill. There is Death with his terrors. And all the air is filled with legions of Principalities and Powers that fight against him.

Turning from them for a moment Paul glances upward. One sight of that Face and they are all forgotten. A whisper of the Master's love and these forces are made powerless; one touch of that Hand and they are gone. Then all the heart within him bursts with rapturous triumph. *"In all these things we are more than conquerors through Him that loved us, for I am persuaded that neither death nor life, nor angels nor principalities, nor things present, nor things to come, nor powers, nor heights, nor depth, nor any other creature shall be able to separate us from the love of God which is in Christ Jesus our Lord."* It is the voice of this love so wonderful, so infinite, so abiding, that speaks to us every one.

Therefore I say unto you, Be not anxious.

THE KING OF LOVE MY SHEPHERD IS
Henry Baker, 1868

❧

The King of love my Shepherd is,
Whose goodness faileth never;
I nothing lack if I am His
And He is mine for ever.

Where streams of living water flow
My ransom'd soul He leadeth,
And, where the verdant pastures grow
With food celestial feedeth.

Perverse and foolish oft I stray'd,
But yet in love He sought me,
And on His shoulder gently laid,
And home, rejoicing, brought me.

In death's dark vale I fear no ill
With Thee, dear Lord, beside me;
Thy rod and staff my comfort still,
Thy Cross before to guide me.

Thou spreads a table in my sight;
Thy unction grace bestoweth;
And oh, what transport of delight
From Thy pure chalice floweth!

And so through all the length of days
Thy goodness faileth never:
Good Shepherd, may I sing Thy praise
Within Thy house for ever.